The Poetry of Annette Breaux

Poetically Speaking:
25 Tips and Poems for Teachers

No Adults Allowed:
35 Lessons and Poems for Teachers and Students

EYE ON EDUCATION
6 DEPOT WAY WEST, SUITE 106
LARCHMONT, NY 10538
(914) 833–0551
(914) 833–0761 fax
www.eyeoneducation.com

Library of Congress Cataloging-in-Publication Data

Breaux, Annette L.
    The poetry of Annette Breaux.
        p. cm.
    ISBN 1-930556-92-6
    1. Education—Poetry. 2. Poetry—Study and teaching. I. Ti-
tle.
    PS3602.R43P64 2005
    811'.6—dc22

                                        2004015840

10 9 8 7 6 5 4 3 2

Editorial and production services provided by:
Richard H. Adin, Freelance Editorial Services
52 Oakwood Blvd., Poughkeepsie, NY 12603-4112
(845) 471-3566

Dedication

To Elizabeth, Andrée, Paul, and Denise—my siblings, my lifelines, and my four best friends. Thanks for always keeping the "child" in me alive. I love you more than life itself.

Foreword

My poetry has been a part of me for as long as I can remember. And though I have always enjoyed writing it, I have typically kept it to myself. In recent years, I began sharing bits and pieces of it with educators during my speeches. Invariably, it seemed that no matter what else I had to say during my presentations, teachers always wanted copies of the poetry, wanting to know if I had a book of poems. So I have listened to my fellow educators and finally compiled what you now hold. I hope you enjoy reading them as much as I enjoyed writing them.

But first, consider yourself duly warned…

Warning!

If you dare to read this book, I give you this fair warning
You will not be the same when you wake up in the
    morning
You'll see the whole wide world from a different point of
    view
Your friends and neighbors may not even recognize you
So think before you read; be careful before you act
Because once you do, you'll read it through
And that, my friend, is a fact.

Annette L. Breaux

This volume includes two books. Book One, "Poetically Speaking," provides helpful tips for teachers along with corresponding poems. These tips and poems are designed to be thought provoking and to help us, as teachers, take a good look and often have a good laugh at ourselves. Yes, we all know that we should be more positive, that we should smile more, that we should practice patience with the students we teach, and all that other good stuff. But the fact remains that teaching is tough and that students continually try our patience. They do it on purpose! It's a conspiracy! So hopefully, these tips and poems will help you to rise above the insurgency and deal more effectively with the challenges of the classroom.

Book Two, "No Adults Allowed," is designed for use with the students in your classroom—students of ALL ages. Although each is written from the viewpoint of a child, the lessons are universal, applying to 5-year-olds and 95-year-olds alike. They are rich in wisdom and are used successfully in college classrooms and in elementary classrooms, on the football field, and in the band room.

For Book Two, there is a lesson provided with each poem, and it is recommended that you, the teacher, share the poems with your students and discuss the lessons within. However, please understand that each *lesson* only gives my interpretation and meaning of each poem. I encourage you to allow your students to find their own meanings within each poem, as each student is likely to derive personal meaning based on his own life experiences. Also, use your own judgment to adapt the lessons to the age and maturity levels of your students.

Finally, I offer my genuine appreciation to all my fellow teachers. Your work is nobler than you will ever fully realize. You are important, and your wisdom, guidance, and knowledge are so desperately needed by your students—those precious, aggravating, loving, contriving, huggable little contradictions of themselves. Each of them is someone special. Each deserves a caring, capable, competent teacher—a teacher who believes that the students can, insists that they do, and picks them up when they don't. Thank you for being that "person" to the students you teach. Thank you for making a difference!

Book One

Poetically Speaking:

25 Tips and Poems
for Teachers

Tip 1

Smile often. Students respond to happy teachers, as they feel less threatened and more accepted and respected. If you doubt this, go into your classroom tomorrow and make a conscious effort to smile all day long. Okay, smile most of the time. Well, at least smile more than you're accustomed to smiling... Your own happiness will be contagious. You'll even trick your own brain into thinking that you're happier than you actually are. Seriously, this has been proven by scientific research! When you smile, your brain releases endorphins that make you happier—even if your smile is fake! So fake it if you must, but start smiling, notice the difference in your students, and you'll be a believer! And a happy believer at that!

To Smile or Not to Smile

I am a brand new teacher
Who's been told to hide my smile
And it's clear that the teacher who told me that
Hasn't smiled in quite a while
With lines so deeply etched in her brow
It seems that there's no turning back now
Like her, I do not wish to be
So I'm trying to ignore her advice to me

And I notice that none of her students
Respond to her very kindly
They run out of her classroom each day
When the bell rings, screaming "Finally!"

So smile I will and successful I'll be
A happy teacher my students will see
For happy students behave, I'm told
And miserable teachers grow miserably old.

Tip 2

Encourage your students to take risks and make mistakes. Remind them that we learned to ride a bike by falling at first. And when we fell, our parents said, "Great! Get right back up and try again." I can assure you that *none* of our parents, the first time we fell, put a sign on our foreheads that said, "Non-bike rider!" By falling, we learned how not to fall. And so it is with anything that we learn. The lesson lies within the fall.

And so, teachers, remind yourselves and your students that it's okay to fall often and fall hard. The lesson learned is the reward.

Worth the Risk

I gave an incorrect answer
And you thanked me for taking a chance
You said that by my courage
My knowledge would surely advance
I could have felt embarrassed
But you handled it so well
You reached your hand out just in time
And caught me before I fell
So not only am I still standing
But I'm standing tall and proud
And next time, even if I'm not sure
I'll be willing to risk it aloud.

Tip 3

Greet your students daily as if you are genuinely glad to see them. Students behave much better in environments where they feel needed and wanted. So do adults. That's why we're greeted at Wal-Mart, in a restaurant, on an airplane, etc. The fact is that happy customers become repeat customers who are willing to buy what you are selling. Likewise, happy students come back each day willing to buy what you're teaching. Therein lies your wealth! (Thank goodness, because your paycheck possibly falls a little short of "wealth" status!)

Be Nice

Good morning to you and how do you do
I'm glad that you're here today
That's how our very most favorite teacher
Greets us every day
But down the hall, we're all appalled
As we enter that dreaded room
Where Mrs. "Preacher," our least favorite teacher
Flies in on her broom
Hurry up—get to your seats
Get busy right away
No kind hello, not even for "show"
Just torture day after day
So we, in kind, just close our minds
And we treat her with disrespect
She's always angry anyway
What else can she expect?
So though we may be only kids
We offer these words of advice
Teachers, if you want to reach us—
You will if you'll just be nice!

Tip 4

Avoid "power struggles" with students at all costs. They're pointless, they're futile, and they make you appear unprofessional. The second you engage in a power struggle with a student, you lose. You lose your professionalism and you lose the respect of your students.

You will notice that the poem, though fun in nature, is symbolic of a power struggle. It goes nowhere and basically says nothing and accomplishes nothing. So it is with power struggles—a lot said and nothing accomplished. Therefore, even though you "can," please "don't."

If I Could

If I could, then I would
Whether or not you think I should
I wouldn't because I couldn't
Not because you think I shouldn't
But I can't so I won't
And since I won't then I don't
Now should you feel confused
Or should you feel amused?
Since you won't tell me what I should
Then I won't tell you—but I could!

Tip 5

Do not procrastinate. As teachers, we face mountains of paperwork on a daily basis. However, if you've ever climbed a mountain—which I have not, but I'm imagining here— I'm assuming that when you get to the top, you do not want to climb a second or third until you have had time to catch your breath. One mountain at a time, please! So, teachers, tackle one mountain every day and you'll never get behind. As tempting as it may be to let it go at times, keep up with your paperwork, your lesson plans, your grading, and yes, your sanity! Again, do not procrastinate. It's much better to be on top of your workload than to have your workload on top of you!

I'll Do it Tomorrow

I didn't feel like doing it
So I put it off for a day
And the next day came and I put off more
Too much was coming my way
I used up tons of paper
With my list of "things to do"
And every day my list of things
Just grew and grew and grew
It overtook my kitchen
Then it overtook my house
It overtook my children
And it overtook my spouse
If only I had done the things
That needed to be done
It would have been much easier
To do things one by one
But now I'm overwhelmed
With all the things I have to do
How will I survive this?
I do not have a clue!
And sitting atop these things to do
Are feelings of guilt and sorrow
So I'm turning over a new leaf.
Yep, I'll do it tomorrow!

Tip 6

Make each lesson "real" for your students. This means taking each new skill or bit of information and making it relate to the real-life experiences of your students. For instance, if you're teaching students the importance of "adjectives," have them tell you about their favorite outfits without using any descriptive words. And every time they accidentally use a descriptive word, stop them. Soon enough, they will realize that adjectives help them to communicate more clearly with others. Students can relate to this. They cannot, however, relate to writing the definition of an adjective, doing Exercise A in the textbook, and underlining all of the descriptive words—at least not until they recognize that "adjectives" affect their daily lives and that without them, life would be much more difficult. This, teachers, is real-life teaching! Make it "real" for your students and "real" learning will abound!

Make it Real

I just don't see the point in why I need to know this
   junk
You say if I don't learn it, then surely I will flunk
But I need a better reason for learning all this stuff
It's boring and it's pointless, so learning it is rough
And every time I'm bored in school, I think of other
   things
Lost inside a daydream until the school bell rings
Which means I haven't learned it, which means my
   grades are bad
Which means that I'm in trouble and my mom and
   dad are mad
And then I get so far behind that it's just too late
   to pass
So next year here I am again—I'm right back in your
   class
I didn't get it last year—I don't get it today
Please, teacher, make it real for me so that I can
   move on in May!

Tip 7

Avoid homework overload. Students are in school all day long. The last thing they want to do when they get home is more schoolwork. And by the way, the last thing you want to do when you get home is more schoolwork! But hey, it's part of your job... Kids, however, deserve to have at least some time for just being kids. So when you do assign homework, keep that in mind. Make the homework brief and meaningful.

A parent recently said to me, "I guess my child will have to wait until he's grown before he can just be a kid." She then explained that her son, a seventh-grader and an "A" student, came home from school every day with typically one and a half to two hours of homework every night. And this was an "A" student! Imagine the kids who struggle academically! Remember, teachers: Give them a break—their childhoods are at stake!

The Life of a Kid

Go to school all the day
Do your homework before you play
Be sure to be in bed by eight
Up at dawn, do not be late
Tonight inside my bed I lay
A very selfish prayer I pray
I beg and plead with Mr. Sun
Shine longer tomorrow—I need to have fun!

Tip 8

Refrain from lecturing by getting students actively involved in lessons. The fact is that idle students are either misbehaving or sleeping, neither of which is desirable behavior in a classroom. Another fact is that lecturing will not ignite or excite your students. Get them involved. Wear them out. Remember that the one who's doing the doing is the only one who's doing the learning!

Teach Away

Teach, teach, teach away
Preach, preach all the day
You'd save your voice and I'd learn more, too
If you'd stop talking and let me do!

Tip 9

Believe that your students can, and they will! Students tend to rise to our expectations of them. Show me a teacher who believes in students and I'll show you a classroom of successful students. That, of course, does not mean that they are all achieving at the same levels. They're not.

A teacher recently shared the following: "I had a student who was so far behind and so lacking in motivation that I just wanted to throw the towel in, but, of course, I didn't. At the end of the year, following his phenomenal academic and social growth, he thanked me for believing in him. I almost felt guilty because I knew that I had not believed in him at first. But the one thing I did was pretended to believe in him, and it worked! So my advice to teachers is that if you really don't believe in your students, fake it. It works!" Try it, teachers. By believing in your students, they'll make believers out of you!

Believe in me

I didn't understand, but my teacher just moved on

She said she had no time to wait for the light on me to
dawn

So on she moved and there I stayed; she left me in the
dust

The idea that I was capable was one she did not trust

How far would I have gone had she given me her all

Had she just reached out her hand to me and not just
let me fall

I guess I'll never really know, but I know it's not too late

I have a brand new teacher now who has not sealed my
fate

She says that I can do it; we work until I do

She's patient and determined. She believes in me. Do
you?

Tip 10

Please do not, at any cost, yell and scream at students. Yes, they'll aggravate you. Yes, they'll try your patience. But no, you cannot afford to lose your professionalism. We are, as teachers, supposed to be modeling for our students how to maintain self control in even the toughest of situations. We want our students to see, by our actions, that it is possible and productive to possess control over our emotions. We want—we need—for them to carry this lesson into their own lives. This is not to say that you don't discipline a student who is doing something inappropriate. It is to say, rather, that you discipline students in a self-disciplined way. Yelling and screaming only serve to make you appear unprofessional and out of control. Do not engage in the expression of rage, 'cause you'll lose your cool and look like a fool!

Lost Within a Shout

You yelled at me and I yelled back—What else was there
   to do?

We yelled some more and our throats got sore, and the
   tension grew and grew

And finally, in exhaustion, we both ran out of steam

Left standing in embarrassment, no pride left to redeem

What point is there in thinking that being "right" we must

And pushing on till all involved just lose respect and
   trust?

Maybe if we'd listened, we could have met half way

Let's talk next time and really hear what the other has
   to say

For if we both could do that, maybe we'd find out

That never has a point been made when lost within a
   shout!

Tip 11

Inspire your students with everything you are and everything you have to give. To inspire means to influence by example. Therefore, if you want your students to want and love to learn, then you have to make sure they see how much you want and love to teach. Your enthusiasm will spark theirs. The fact is that we can get more inspiration from an exciting person who has very little to say than we can from a boring person who has lots to say.

So take the best from both of those. Be an exciting teacher who has lots to say, and your students will amaze you every single day!

An Ounce of Inspiration

Give me an ounce of inspiration—
    leading, of course, to motivation
Which will spark my imagination
    Thus, you'll see my perspiration
As I feel my mind's vibration—
    spurring on my new creation
Concentration for the duration
    Whew! I did it! Pure elation!

Tip 12

Never underestimate the power of your influence. I recently attended a funeral of a 92-year-old woman who had taught for many years. The minister who conducted the ceremony was a former student of hers. He thanked her for his vocation. The congregation was full of former students, all of whom owed much of their successes in life to this teacher. One student shared that she used to come to school even when she was burning with fever, because she was not about to miss the excitement in that class-room even for a day. Even though many of these students had been taught by her over 60 years prior, they could still recount things she said, things they did, and lessons they learned. All of this from one teacher! So many lives touched, so many lessons learned.

As teachers, our influence lives on, today, tomorrow, and long after we are gone.

If I Could Teach My Students

If I could teach my students one solitary thing
A sense of ever-questioning to each one I would bring
And by their curiosity, they'd learn to teach themselves
For the more that one uncovers, the deeper that he
    delves
If as one student's teacher, I light a fire within
Then I have touched the world indeed—
Influence does not end.

Tip 13

Give your students a little more credit than they may deserve, and you'll get a little better than what they were giving. It's called using clever psychology.

A teacher recently approached a student who had trouble getting started on his work every day. Day after day this went on, until finally the teacher decided to use some clever psychology. She went to the student and said, "I've just realized that you're one of those students who has that special gift." He looked at her and asked, "What gift?" She said, "You're one of those rare few who has to form a picture in your mind before you can get started on your work. That's an amazing talent! But hurry and get your mental picture finished so that you can get started putting it all on paper." The student "bought it" and got busy, every day, for the rest of the year. Hey, whatever it takes!

A Very Clever Teacher

We had to draw a picture one day, and I couldn't decide what to draw

So I decided to leave my paper blank, and my teacher looked at it in awe

"What a beautiful, fluffy, white cloud," she said. "May I hang it on the wall?"

And I realized that she did not notice that I had drawn nothing at all

Then she proudly hung for all to see the work I had not done

But with her permission I took it home and I added the sky and the sun

And now that I think about it, I wonder if she really knew

That my drawing was not of a cloud at all—It was work I did not do

I thought that I had tricked her, but maybe it was she

Who used a clever way to get me to draw a picture for all to see.

Tip 14

Plan each lesson with the end result in mind. As teachers, we often get caught up in a "topic" or "theme" when teaching something. We cover a lot of territory, yet the students are not clear on exactly what it is they're supposed to be learning. That's because **we're** not always clear, every day, on exactly what it is we want the students to know or be able to do at the end of each day's lesson. Be sure to have a focus for each lesson and let the students know, at the beginning of each lesson, what they'll be able to do by the end of the lesson. Be very clear and very specific with your lesson objectives.

Know where you're going and know what you want the students to be able to do, and you're all much more likely to reach your destination.

Which Way?

I stood at a fork in the road
And didn't know which way to go
But since I had no destination in mind
If I got there, I'd never know!

Tip 15

Remember to "light a spark" in your students. Make it your utmost priority to set each of them aglow with a desire to work harder, to search for answers, to acquire deeper understandings, to love learning, and to be better people. If you can do that, you have done your job uncommonly well. For it is you, the teacher, who will determine whether your students walk away "ignited" or "extinguished." So set them afire with learning's desire!

I Teach

I light a spark in a darkened soul
I warm the heart of one grown cold
I look beyond and see within
Behind the face, beneath the skin
I quench a thirst, I soothe a pain
I provide the food that will sustain
I touch, I love, I laugh, I cry
Whatever is needed, I supply
Yet more than I give, I gain from each
I am most richly blessed—I teach.

Tip 16

Don't fall into the "woe is me" trap. We've all known them—the teachers who walk around with black clouds hanging over their heads. Nothing good to say, never a smile, never a positive gesture, eternally vile!

No one likes to be in their presence, no one likes to get caught in a conversation with them, and everyone likes to talk about them. And those are just the opinions of the other teachers! Imagine being a student in the classroom of one of these teachers! A painful thought, at best. Needless to say, these are the least effective teachers of all. Of course, it's not their fault! They're victims. Just ask them!

Please, teachers, don't fall into the "woe is me" trap. Teachers who assume this plot are never respected but easy to spot.

Oh Woe Is me

Oh woe is me, I am a teacher
Parent, doctor, therapist, preacher
Battling daily with the youth
Whose attitudes are more than uncouth
A disciplinarian, no stranger to force
Don't talk to me after 3:30—I'm hoarse
One year of experience twenty times o'er
I teach each year like the year before
My students are disrespectful and lazy
Yet they look at me like I am crazy
If it weren't for students, my life would be swell
And my job wouldn't seem like a living hell
Speaking of which, I've gotta go
My principal's coming—gotta put on a show!

Tip 17

Remember that in the classroom, children should be seen AND heard. Silent classrooms silence learning. Structured noise is a good thing. The key word here is "structured." Teachers who are excellent classroom managers have classrooms that are constantly "humming" with activity and the joyful sounds of students learning. Teachers who lack management skills tend to insist on absolute silence because they are afraid that the "noise" will get out of hand. Again, silent classrooms silence learning. Here we are, teaching, for instance, the English language in many of our classrooms. And we literally have teachers attempting to teach that language in silence! Just in case you doubt the ineffectiveness of that technique, pick a language, any language, that you do not speak. Now get some tapes or sign up for some classes or whatever, but attempt to learn this new language without actually speaking. Need I say more? Nope, but your students should probably be saying more in your classrooms!

A Golden Noise

Noise is golden when children are heard
Excitement exuding from each spoken word
Questioning everything as children do
Uncovering answers, discovering what's new
And oh so joyful to play some small part
I teach the children—I touch the heart!

Tip 18

Encourage students' questions. Yes, one of the most frustrating things for teachers is to have to be constantly answering so many different questions from so many different students every single day. However, just as answering questions is part of the job of teaching, asking questions is part of the job of learning! The fact that they're asking says that we have them wondering. Children who are in a state of wondering are also in a state of learning. And as tempting as it may be, stay away from phrases such as "Now you know that's not a serious question," or "I just answered that question for someone else." or "Where were you when we discussed that yesterday? You should know the answer to that question," or "If you'd stop asking so many questions, maybe I could teach you something!" Okay, you get the point.

And so, teachers, encourage students' questions. Don't discourage them and squelch them.

Too Many Questions

You say I ask too many questions
But you just don't seem to see
That I wonder about so many things
For which answers there surely must be
But once I know an answer
A new question grows in my mind
Because what I learn uncovers
New problems with answers to find
So be patient with my questioning
There still is so much I don't know
But I do know that learning more answers
Will certainly help me to grow.

Tip 19

Take a good look at yourself before being quick to find fault with others. In any profession where a group of people work closely together as do teachers, there are always a select few who are more than willing to assume the self-appointed roles of "fault finders." They're quick to point out everything that others do wrong, even though those "others" are also doing many things right. They continue to find fault with others despite the fact that they, too, have many faults of their own. It happens between teachers and it happens between teachers and students. But please, teachers, make a concerted effort to avoid that type of behavior. Instead, realize that it never hurts and always helps to find less "fault" and notice more "good" in others.

And so, teachers, find the good and praise it. Their self-esteem? You'll raise it!

A Look in the Mirror

If I could just deal with everyone else
    and not have to deal with me
Life would be good, as I know I could
    be a wonderful "Dear Abby"
But having to deal with my stuff isn't easy—
    it's actually very hard
For dealing with only my "stuff," I guess
    I would never receive an award
It's easy to give advice, you see—
    and actually I'm quite good
But I don't always follow my own advice
    though I know that I really should
So I'm starting to look in the mirror today
    and I'll deal with the one looking back
And I'll stop trying to find fault with everyone else
    to make up for whatever I lack.

Tip 20

Remember that our perceptions of students are not always accurate. The fact is that if we knew the real stories behind our students, our perceptions of them would change drastically, and we would treat them quite differently. Our perceptions of others are rarely accurate. We cannot assume to be mind readers or to know what goes on in other people's lives. Often, we label students by their outward behaviors neglecting to find out what, on the inside, is causing those behaviors. How often do some teachers hear about the successes of former students only to say, "Wow! I'm amazed he went that far in life. I didn't know he had it in him." Well, the reason they didn't "know" was that their set perceptions blinded them from seeing what was there all along.

Don't be so set in your perceptions of others. Always assume you don't really know them, and usually you'll be right. Give every student the fighting chance that he deserves!

I'm Not the One You Think You Know

If you could see what I can see
Then you would see me differently
I see from here, you see from there
Perception differs everywhere
I'm not the one you think you know
So please let that perception go.

Tip 21

Never forget that students tend to take us at our word. They really do believe what we tell them. If we say, "You're just not a good math student and probably never will be," then guess what? They probably never will be. The problem here is twofold: On the one hand, our negative statements are internalized by the student, and on the other hand, our negative beliefs influence our actions toward that student. We believe he can't, so we never expect him to. Nor do we ever tell him that he can. The good news is that the opposite is also true. Positive statements are internalized by a student, and our positive beliefs influence our actions toward that student.

Be realistic, of course, but don't underestimate any student's ability to achieve. Tell him he can, and he just might!

Tell Me I Can Do it

You said I couldn't do it
I believed just what you said
So I simply didn't try it
The desire then left my head
And as I think about it
I wonder how you can know
What I can and can't accomplish
How I will or will not grow
But I'm just a little kid, you see,
I believe just what you say
Tell me I can do it
And maybe I will someday!

Tip 22

Give students explicit directions for any and all tasks. This involves telling them exactly what to do, how to do it, when to do it, why to do it, how much to do, how well to do it, etc. Don't assume that they know or that they'll figure it out. Students resent having to "figure out" what it is the teacher expects of them. Typical confusion from students sounds like this: "Do we have to write the definitions? Do we need to read the whole chapter? Can we just put the answers to the problems or do we have to show our work? How many can we get wrong and still pass?" If these questions sound all too familiar, you may want to consider the fact that you're probably not being specific enough.

Be specific, because the more specific you are, the more your students will understand exactly what it is you want from them, and the better will be your chances of receiving quality work.

Too Much, Not Enough

Too short, too tall, too big, too small
Too hot, too cold, too young, too old
Too loose, too tight, too wrong, too right
Too smooth, too rough, too much, not enough
Too weak, too strong, too short, too long
Too skinny, too fat, too this, too that
Too early, too late, too crooked, too straight
Too dark, too light—Enough? Not quite.
Too good, too bad, too happy, too sad
Too high, too low—Yes? No.
Too fragile, too tough
Is this poem long enough?

Tip 23

Remember to find the good in every student and praise it as often as possible. Mark Twain once said, "I can live for two months on a good compliment." He spoke for us all. Nothing urges us onward like a little praise. So praise good behavior in the classroom if you want to see more of it, and praise it often. There's plenty good going on in every classroom. Don't get so caught up in the negatives that you forget to notice the good. Every student has characteristics worthy of praise. Every student has characteristics worthy of criticism. By recognizing and focusing on the positives, you'll defuse, if not eliminate, the negatives. Praise the positives often, and watch the negatives soften!

A Little Praise

I helped a girl at school one day
Who had fallen and scraped her knee
I only did what any kid would've done
If they were me
Then the teacher said that I was one
Of the nicest kids she'd met
And I thought to myself,
"Well that's because she doesn't know me yet"
'Cause I'm really not so nice sometimes
I say and do bad things
I don't always finish my homework
Or come in right when the bell rings
But my teacher keeps on thinking
That I'm really extra nice
So whenever I'm around her
I'm nice, not once, but twice
I even work much harder
When I am in her class
Instead of going really slow
I finish extra fast
She always takes the time to notice
Everything good that I do
She's told me I'm special so many times
That I think it's becoming true.

Tip 24

Remember that if your students knew all the answers, your services would no longer be needed. I recently spoke with a nervous teacher who was about to be observed by her principal. She said to me, "I'll call on only the students whom I'm sure will answer correctly." I replied by saying, "Well, I guess you can count on failing that observation." In shock, she replied, "What do you mean?" I then explained that if an observer observes a lesson where students know all of the answers, that observer will note that the teacher should not have been wasting her time teaching something the students already knew. Once we determine that our students understand a concept, we should immediately move on to something new and more challenging. "You see," I explained, "if your students knew all of the answers, then you would be out of a job." The teacher, now considerably relieved, went on to do an excellent job with her students who did not know all the answers. It's called teaching!

Because of Us

I don't get all the answers right
And my teacher thinks I'm not too bright
Which puts more pressure on my mind
And makes the answers hard to find
And here I thought that students were not
    supposed to know it all
I thought that teachers were there to help
    us up each time we'd fall
Teacher, if we never fell at all, then you'd be
    working at the mall
For without our lack of knowledge, there'd
    be no teaching degree in college
So I guess that what I'm trying to say—
    is be grateful we don't yet know the way
Welcome our ignorance and never fear
Because of us, you have a career!

And finally, teachers…

Tip 25

Never forget to look behind the masks that children so often wear… It has often been said that if we knew the true story behind each misbehaving child, then nine times out of ten we'd be heartbroken instead of angry. That is not to say that we should ignore the misbehavior. Rather it means that we should approach it a little less emotionally and a lot more sensibly. In other words, we should attack the problem and help the person. Look behind the mask and see what's hiding there. A student will remove the mask once he believes you care about the real person hidden back there.

Behind the Mask

If you could see inside of me
Then surely you would know
That beneath my bad behavior
Is a kid who needs you so
I need to feel your love for me
I need your caring smile
I need to feel important each day
If only for a while
I need for all your wisdom
To pour out onto me
It might not sink in right away
But one day it will, you'll see
I need a lot of patience
I need a calming voice
I need someone to show me how
To make a better choice
I know it won't be easy
I'll push and test you often
But surely, teacher, you must know
That hard hearts can be softened
So see me as your challenge,
Your calling, and your task
And search until you've found the good
That's hidden behind the mask.

Book Two

No Adults Allowed:

35 Lessons and Poems for Teachers and Students

Lesson 1

Discuss with students the importance that we often put on physical beauty and outward appearances while neglecting the fact that true beauty comes from within. How others view us from the "outside" is not enough to make us happy. We have to feel good about ourselves and be good people on the "inside." Just as a beautiful house on the "outside" is not necessarily a happy home on the "inside," a beautiful person on the "outside" is not necessarily a happy or good person on the "inside." And the most important thing is who we are on the inside. That's where real beauty lies.

This could extend into a discussion of whether or not students think all "models" or "movie stars" are good people on the inside due to the fact that they're physically appealing on the outside. Again, culminate the discussion by drawing them back to the real lesson—it's how beautiful we are on the inside that really counts!

I Drew a Pretty Picture

I drew a pretty picture
Of a house with flowers and trees
Then the door to the house opened
And I heard "Come in, please."
"Who, me?" I asked
"Yes, you," it laughed
"Aren't you the one who drew me?"
"Well, yes," I said, "I drew you
but I did not know you knew me."
"Well, come along," the drawing said
"There is no need to worry.
You forgot to draw my inside,
So draw it. Will you? Hurry!"

Lesson 2

The lesson in this poem is evident within the poem. Have students think about the fact that without sadness, we would not be able to recognize happiness. Discuss the "opposites" included in the poem and let them also come up with some of their own. Life is truly a series of ups and down. And opposites are necessary to life's lessons.

Opposites

How could I know what happiness is
If I'd never experienced sadness?
And how could I know I was sad
If I had never experienced gladness?
How could I recognize safety
If I'd never experienced fright?
And how would I know it was daytime
If I'd never experienced night?
I think I'm understanding now
Why opposites exist
I realize that without them
All life's lessons I'd have missed.

Lesson 3

Discuss with students that any situation is determined by our perception of it. Two people can derive two totally different experiences from exactly the same situation... For instance, a child who wants to go swimming may be upset because it's raining whereas the farmer down the road is grateful that his crops are getting some much-needed water. Same rain, two different perspectives. Allow students to discuss situations that might be perceived differently by different people or groups of people. This can even be related to a situation where someone donates his organs to science. He dies, and his family, of course, is grieving. On the other side of that, another family is celebrating because their family member will receive the heart transplant that will save his life. The possibilities for discussion with this poem are endless.

Point of View

I went to my new school today
And when I met my teacher
I noticed something unusual
As I studied his every feature
Was it his eyes? Was it his nose?
His hair was nice enough
"Get in your seats!" he bellowed
His tone a little rough
The boy who sat behind me said
"I've never seen such a frown!"
But since I was standing on my head
He had the nicest smile around.

Lesson 4

This poem is simply about the absolute magic of friendship. It's a perfect opportunity to discuss the importance of having friends and of being a true friend to others. It is also an opportunity to discuss how to determine which people in your life are truly your friends. The topic of "peer pressure" would be appropriate here also in determining that people who push us to do things that are wrong or bad are not our true friends. Yet another discussion could be the proper treatment of animals.

The Magic of Friendship

I found a bird with a broken wing
Which I thought to be quite tragic
I brought him home, not knowing
That this little bird was magic
As soon as we were in my room
He began to sing
And with his song of magic words
He healed his broken wing
He flew onto my shoulder
And kissed me on the cheek
"What's that for?" I asked him
As I stroked his tiny beak
"For caring enough to take me home,"
he said, "so I could mend.
Magic works much better
When it's shared with a friend."

Lesson 5

This poem is about having empathy for others, especially those who are ostracized. Students of all ages can relate to this poem. Have them share their own experiences where either they were able to empathize with someone else or someone else was able to empathize with them.

This poem is also about the power of teamwork—working in accord with others to achieve a common goal—which will make for another interesting discussion with students.

Choosing Sides

We got to pick teams for softball today
And I got to do the choosing
So I picked all the people that anyone else
Would've picked if they planned on losing
I picked the ones who never got picked
Or at least not picked until last
The ones who got put in positions
Where no fly balls ever passed
I knew that the deed I was doing
Was well worth losing the game
To see pride on the very same faces
That were usually filled with shame
The other kids thought I was crazy
They asked if I knew what I'd done
But while they got cocky and lazy
We worked as a team and won.

Lesson 6

This poem provides an opportunity to discuss with students the fact that children are often torn between wanting to be independent and needing to be dependent. For instance, children often want to make their own decisions and to be left alone by adults. That is, until it's suppertime or until they need a ride somewhere or they need spending money, etc. This is a natural part of growing up.

Discuss some of the purposes that adults serve in the lives of children. And discuss the fact that the older we get, the more decisions we make on our own. But the process is gradual. Take time to discuss some levels of both "dependency" and "independency" that would be appropriate to the age and/or maturity levels of your students.

No Adults Allowed

I built myself a club house
When I finished I felt quite proud
Especially of the sign which read
"No Adults Allowed"
I stayed inside for a very long time
My mom said that I could
I bet, though, when she said that
She didn't think I would
The minutes turned to hours
The day soon turned to night
I heard a noise, my hair stood up
My eyes were wide with fright
"Who's there?" I asked, but no reply
So I screamed, "Mom, please come get me!"
"I can't," I heard my mom say
"I'm an adult and you won't let me."
"Please," I begged, and Mom inquired,
"What do you want, Thomas?"
"Just come inside and get me.
I'll change the sign, I promise."

Lesson 7

This is a "fun" poem pointing out that we all exist from a "me" standpoint and experience everything from within. This makes us all alike in many ways. Sometimes, we seem to forget just how much alike we all really are. Have students discuss ways that we are all alike—for instance, we all need the love and support of others, we all have hopes and dreams, we all struggle with similar emotions, etc.

Hey, You!

"Hey, you!" he said, and looked at me
My reply, to him, confusing
"I'm not you, I'm me, you're you
Your mind you must be losing."
"Hey," he said, "I'm not you
I am me, too
So if I'm me, and if you're me
Then who in the world is you?"

Lesson 8

We, as teachers, should recognize that old adages, sayings, clichés, etc. are not understood by most children. The child in this poem is taking those sayings literally just as children often take us literally. Here is a perfect chance to explain to students what it means when we say things like "The grass isn't always greener on the other side of the fence," or "I'll give them a piece of my mind," etc. Explain one saying at a time and have students determine how it relates to their own life experiences. You may also want to discuss other sayings not included in the poem. Another example would be the saying "Every rose has its thorns."

Things That Don't Make Sense to Me

If the grass isn't really greener on the other side of
the fence
Does that mean we're color blind? Or are we all just
dense?

If it really doesn't matter who wins or loses in score
Then why do we have scoreboards, and what in the
world are they for?

Mom says that in due time, I'll develop a taste for
spinach
I already have—a bad one—so take it away, please,
I'm finished!

If happiness comes from giving a thing and never
comes when you get it
Then who in the world can I give it to? If they take it,
won't they regret it?

If life is a bowl of cherries, then doesn't it seem unfair
That those who don't like cherries are doomed to a
life of despair?

If I give you a piece of my mind, does that make you
smarter than I?
'Cause if it does, I'll keep my thoughts and think
them on the sly!

So many things I wonder about, and most just
don't make sense
Therefore if the grass looks greener to me, that's it —
I'm crossing the fence!

Lesson 9

This poem is about the fact that most of us are rarely content with our current states. It lends itself to an excellent discussion on the fact that kids tend to want to be adults and adults tend to yearn for their youth. Discuss, with your students, what would happen if they truly could trade places with adults. Lead them to see that they are not yet knowledgeable or skillful or experienced enough to take on the responsibilities of adults by discussing some of the responsibilities that adults have. If children could realize the kinds of responsibilities that adults face on a daily basis, they would very likely choose to hold on to childhood as long as possible.

Trading Places

"Wipe that look off your face, young lady!"
Our moms say as they fuss us
Okay, we have a great idea!
We know it will work, trust us.
Kids want to be old, adults want to be young
So why don't we just trade places?
Then we can tell the adults what to do
And they can make the faces.

Lesson 10

This poem makes for an excellent discussion on bullying. Bullies tend to pick on people younger, smaller, or more vulnerable than themselves. When they meet their matches, they're not so tough after all. Discuss, with your students, what makes some people bully others—their lack of self confidence, their inner turmoil, their sense of powerlessness in life, etc. The fact is that when students begin to understand what make bullies "tick," they're less intimidated by them. And when "bullies" understand what causes them to be bullies, they're much less likely to continue the bullying.

Go Away, Bully

I'm just a little kid
And I don't fight well
So go away, big bully
If you don't, I'll have to tell
And telling is the last thing
you want for me to do
'Cause it gets you into trouble
  with someone even bigger than you.

Lesson 11

From time to time, we all come up with excuses in order to put off one thing when we'd rather be doing something else. But often times, we expend more energy thinking of ways to get out of doing something than it would take to just actually do the thing and be done with it. Any student can relate to this poem. Have them share experiences of their own procrastinating tendencies along with lessons learned the hard way from putting important tasks off until the last minute.

Who Took My Homework?

I can't find my homework
But I'm sure that I did it
Maybe little sister found a hiding place
And hid it
Rover likes paper
So maybe he ate it
Doing me a favor
'Cause he knows how much I hate it
Maybe a great wind came and blew it far away
I'll probably find it outside
When I go out to play
"What? I can't go outside, you say
until I do it?"
So much for excuses
I guess this time I blew it.

Lesson 12

This poem is about the power of books and their ability to spark our creativity, awaken our curiosity, feed our imaginations, and touch our hearts. The age levels of students you are teaching will guide this discussion. Yet regardless of whether you are teaching 5-year-olds or 18-year-olds, books are magical for all. You may also want to discuss with your students the importance of being able to read in today's world.

Fall Inside

Whenever I read a really good book
I cannot put it down
Lots of things go on around me
But I do not hear a sound
I get lost inside of the story
And I actually feel that I'm there
Living with all of the characters
In a place far away somewhere
So if you need to escape sometimes
There's a wonderful place to hide
Just find a good book and start reading
And soon you'll fall inside.

Lesson 13

Kids can sometimes act cruelly by teasing others. The kid in this poem defuses the kid who's teasing him with a very clever response. The message is that though we cannot control how others treat us, we can always control the way we react to them. This poem makes for a potentially endless discussion with students of all ages about the act of teasing and its detrimental effects on others. It also provides the teacher with the opportunity to show students how to "defuse" people who tease them.

Teasing

I don't see as well with my eyes
As you can see with your eyes
And so I got some glasses
And now you call me "Four Eyes"
But that doesn't even make sense
If you really stop to think
Because even when I wear my glasses
I only have two eyes to blink
You call me names to displease me
Which makes you look like a brat
But if you really must tease me
You can surely do better than that.

Lesson 14

   This poem goes beyond the importance of a healthy diet. It is about our uncanny ability to rationalize our actions, even when our actions are not in our best interest. Adults typically do know what's best for children. They're not just trying to aggravate them, though this is not always clear to children... Have your students share with you some of the things they tend to rationalize, even though these things might not be in their best interest. Their experiences will vary depending on their age levels.

Eat Your Vegetables

"Be sure to eat your vegetables
They're good for you, you know
They'll give you such a gleaming smile
They'll help your bones to grow."
Well I'm thinking that my smile's okay
Just the way it is today
And if I grow to be too tall
I'll only have farther to go when I fall
So if I have to stay this way
I will not mind, I'll be just fine
Ice cream, pizza, burgers with cheese
Would you pass the ketchup, please?

Lesson 15

It is very difficult to maintain self-control in the face of anger. But if we do, we have everything to gain. Discuss with students the kinds of things that make them want to lose control. Then discuss alternatives we all have when faced with a loss of control. Sometimes, children don't know a better way. It's our job, as adults and role models, to teach them ways of maintaining control even in the toughest of situations.

Self-Control

Someone made me mad today
and I'm wanting to unload
My temperature is boiling hot
and I feel like I'll explode
My face is really red right now
and my veins are sticking out
I bet I would feel better
if I'd kick and scream and shout
But I'm thinking if I did that
I'd look as bad as they
And I'm sure that I'd regret it
if I said what I'd like to say
So I'm trying to calm myself right now
I'm giving it all I've got
'Cause if I maintain self-control
I will have gained A LOT!

Lesson 16

This poem is a reminder about how we tend to sometimes "wish" our lives away, forgetting to enjoy life here and now. As young children, we can't wait to start school for the first time. Then we're always wishing we were in the next grade level. In high school, we're wishing we were in college. In college, we're wishing we were out on our own, making our own livings and raising our own families, and on and on and on. Discuss with students the kinds of things they "can't wait" for. Let them know that it's okay and also important in life to look forward to things, as long as we don't forget to enjoy ourselves here and now.

An added meaning here is a more literal one. We often seem to wish for things we don't have. For instance, during the school year, nothing looks better to us than summertime. And then during the summer, we tend to get bored and wish we were back in school. Again, this leads us back to the importance of enjoying each day and making the most of our lives here and now.

Counting the Days

I can't wait for school to end
Summertime is near
Swimming, playing, sleeping late
Counting the days till it's here
But a few weeks into summer
I've slept and played and swum
And life is on the verge of getting
Boring and humdrum
So I can't wait for school to start
The time is drawing near
New clothes, new friends, new learning begins
Counting the days till it's here.

Lesson 17

The lesson here is that everything is relative. The old saying, "I complained because I had no shoes until I met a man who had no feet" applies here. The fact is that no matter how bad things may seem, they could always be worse. And for someone else, they usually are. Children of all ages can relate to this poem and its meaning. Allow them to discuss ways that other people are not as fortunate as they are.

My Teeth Are Falling

My teeth are falling, left and right
I smile, and it's an awful sight
But Grandpa says it could be worse
At least these teeth are just my first!

Lesson 18

The lesson here is that it's not the gift, but the love within the giving that really matters. Every student, and every person, can relate to opening a present that they would not have chosen for themselves. Have them share some of their stories and then discuss the fact that it is truly the gesture, the thought, and the love behind the giving that are most important.

Opening a Present

I'm opening a present
That I know I will not like
It's not a toy to bring me joy
It's not a brand new bike
I know just what it is inside
My cousin slipped and told me
If my dismay I do not hide
I know my mom will scold me
Aunt Sally looks at Mom and says
"I didn't know what to get her"
Just as I am lifting from the box
A blue-green sweater
"Wow!" I say, "I love it,
I cannot wait to wear it"
I hold my disappointment down
Though it's difficult to bear it
But later on when we get home
I'll have to tell my mother
That because she made me be so nice
Next year I'll get another.

Lesson 19

The lesson here is the beauty of unconditional love. In actuality, if humans loved one another as unconditionally as animals love us, life would be wonderful. Allow students to tell you about their pets and relate to the poem. Even students who do not have pets can relate to the unconditional love of animals. Our animals are always happy to see us, even if we just walk outside to put out the garbage. They love us and accept us no matter what. And even though not all people are animal lovers, we can all learn from the message of unconditional love.

My Best Friend

I know someone who never gets mad
No matter what I do
Whenever he sees me, he's always glad
And he's always there to talk to
He sits and listens about my day
The bad parts and the good
He gives to me in every way
What a really good friend should
So I have decided that I am one
Of the luckiest people I know
Because I've been blessed with the world's
    best friend
My wonderful dog, Milo.

Lesson 20

Sometimes children feel pressured to fulfill the expectations that they think adults have of them. In actuality, children should strive for being good people and giving their best to whatever they do.

Discuss with students the various expectations they perceive others to have of them. Have them compare these to the expectations they have of themselves. Then discuss the importance of being good people and of always giving their very best to their dreams and endeavors. If they can do that, they'll be successful no matter where their life's choices eventually lead them.

When I Grow Up

When I grow up, what will I be?
There are so many choices
So many adults are guiding me
With so many different voices
A teacher, a doctor, a lawyer, a scholar
Find a new way to make a dollar
So many directions—which way should I go?
It's difficult for a kid to know
But the little voice inside of me
Says simply to be the best I can be.

Lesson 21

This makes for an excellent discussion on the art of compromise. Life is not always black and white. People are not always completely wrong or completely right. And our ideas and beliefs are not the only ones with validity. In relationships with others, we often have to give in a little, be more open-minded and accepting, and practice the art of compromise.

Compromise

I don't agree with your way
You don't agree with mine
But there's a way to work it out
So things will be just fine
I'll walk toward you and you toward me
We'll meet up in the middle
I think it's called a compromise
To both give in a little.

Lesson 22

This poem is simply a fun poem about the logical consequences of our actions. Of course, the lesson goes way beyond just putting the toilet seat down. Discuss the fact that all of our actions have consequences and have students share some of the consequences they have had to face due to their actions, both good and bad. The fact is that we all make choices, and the better our choices, the more positive the consequences.

Put the Seat Down

Someone left the toilet seat up
And guess what? I fell in
But then I realized that that someone was me
I won't do that again.

Lesson 23

If we could teach our students the lessons contained within this poem, what a wonderful world this world would soon become. Have students discuss what it means to "be good to all," to "get up when you fall," and to "not ever lose your yearning." Discuss why these things are important and also discuss what would happen if we did not get up when we fell, if we were not good to others, and if we gave in and lost our yearnings.

Lessons for Life

As my young life's pages are turning
The wisest of lessons I'm learning
     Be good to all
     Get up when you fall
And do not ever lose your yearning.

Lesson 24

The saying "What you do speaks so loudly that I cannot hear what you say" applies perfectly here. Discuss with students the fact that people judge us by our actions. That's how it's possible for even a baby who cannot yet speak or understand language to accurately judge the actions of others.

Give a few examples of how loudly actions speak which might include things such as:

- If a person says he's happy while frowning, we will believe his actions and not his words.

- If someone continually says that they are "honest" and then lies to us, the one action of lying will negate his words.

- If people say that they like you but treat you badly with their actions, you will not believe that they like you very much, and you will be correct.

Then have students provide examples of just how loudly actions speak.

What You Do

I'm trapped inside
    of a baby's body
So I cannot speak just yet
You don't know I can
    but I understand
And I feel all the feelings you get
I can tell when you really want me around
And I can tell when you really don't
I know just when you'll give in to me
And I know just when you won't
I know when your mouth turns upward
And your voice gets sweet and low
That the feeling I'm about to feel
Is the happiest feeling I know
So I guess I know a secret
And the secret is about you
The words you speak mean nothing
Compared to what you do.

Lesson 25

Discuss with students that there are many sides to each of us, some good and some not so good. The fact is that we are all human, and no one is even close to being perfect. We all make mistakes, and we all have times when we are not at our best. You may want to have students describe themselves when they are at their best and then describe themselves when they are at their worst. Then discuss the fact that the important thing is to always strive to be better and to learn to recognize our shortcomings and try to overcome them.

Who Am I?

Am I the person who's good inside
Or am I the one who's bad?
The one who's usually happy
Or the one who's sometimes sad?
Is the real me the one who is helpful
Or the one who's sometimes not?
The one you hug so tightly
Or the one you fuss a lot?
Am I the one who makes you smile
Or the one who makes you frown?
The one who gets loud and obnoxious?
Or the one who does not make a sound?

Just exactly who am I?
Which person should I be?
Since I really don't think that I'm anyone else
I guess all these people are me!

Lesson 26

Discuss with students the fact that feelings, in and of themselves, are not wrong, right, bad, or good. What we do about our feelings, however, falls into the categories of wrong, right, bad, or good. We need to express our feelings, for it is never good to hold them inside, but "how" we express them is very important.

Feelings

Jealousy, sadness, mellowness, madness
All of these feelings I feel
And the more I try to ignore them
The harder they are to conceal
But I try to keep a stiff upper lip
I don't let my feelings show
I smile and say that I'm okay
In hopes that no one will know
But they grow so big inside of me
That soon they must come out
And then at someone I love very dearly
I scream and holler and shout
They say that these feelings are normal
They're feelings we all must feel
And only if we can express them
Can our hearts begin to heal
There's a way, they say, to express yourself
And still maintain control
Just open your heart, calmly say your part
And let your feelings unfold.

Lesson 27

It is simply not true that "names" cannot hurt us. Teasing and name–calling can have devastating effects on us. Lesson? We should never use words to hurt others. Students of all ages will have much to contribute during this discussion.

Sticks and Stones

Sticks and stones can break your bones
But names can't hurt, you see
Well, whoever said that
must've never been called
The name that you called me.

Lesson 28

The lesson here is that things are not always what they appear to be. Neither are people. Discussion with students should begin with "magicians" and how they perform some of their magic tricks. Then the discussion can lead into the fact that things in life are not always what they appear from the outside looking in. For instance, a student may be very nervous about a test and yet come into class announcing to his friends that he doesn't care what grade he makes. Therefore, what he feels on the inside and what he portrays on the outside are not at all the same.

People often hide their true feelings from others for a variety of reasons. Have students discuss some of these possible reasons.

Magic Man

I watched a magician
saw a lady in half
And she continued talking
and soon began to laugh
He put her back together
— she walked out in one piece
You'd think she would have bled a little
or cried a little, at least
He then reached down and pulled a rabbit
from an empty hat
He pulled that hare right out of thin air
Hey, how did he do that?

Lesson 29

The little brother is teaching his big brother a valuable lesson by not fighting back. Discuss with students the fact that when we fight back with someone who has lost control, we stoop to his level and help him to justify his own loss of control. By not fighting back, we leave the angry person with only himself to face and only his feelings with which to deal.

Little Brother

I hit my little brother
Because he made me mad
But I had no idea that his response
Would make me feel so bad
He did not fight, he did not cry
When he received my smack
He turned his head and walked away
How I wish he had fought back
So I'm the one who lost my cool
I'm the one who blew it
I stood there feeling like a fool
I wonder if he knew it...

Lesson 30

The lesson here seems almost "oversimplified," but if everyone would "just be nice" to everyone else, what a better place this world would be! This poem lends itself to a discussion with students about how they can back away from someone who is trying to start trouble. It takes a much bigger person to walk away from a fight than to engage in one. The same applies to teasing, to negative peer pressure, etc. The bigger person is the one who knows how to "just be nice" and "just say no."

Just Be Nice

How can you tell me what I should do
When you are not me and I am not you
You make up the rules which you do not follow
You say I'm a fool with brains that are hollow
And though I'll admit that I am no sage
I am pretty wise for a kid my age
I know the difference between wrong and right
So put up your fists but I will not fight
You're just a kid, too, like all of the rest
So leave me alone; do not be a pest
And maybe for once, you'll take my advice
You'd have friends, too, if you'd just be nice.

Lesson 31

The good old "golden rule" still applies and always will. Discuss the rule, have students interpret it, and talk about the fact that we should treat others no differently than we would expect to be treated.

The Golden Rule

Do unto others just as you
Would like for them to do unto you
Listen with care, but do not dare
To tell someone else what to do
Be gentle and kind, and soon you will find
That they'll be the same way with you.

Lesson 32

The lesson here is that to be ourselves is sometimes difficult in a world that compares us to others. Parents tend to compare their children to one another and even teachers sometimes compare siblings that they have taught. It is extremely detrimental to a child to expect him to be anyone but himself. Discuss with students the fact that even though it is good to have role models and to strive constantly to be better people, we must never forget to be ourselves. If we were supposed to have been anyone but ourselves, then we would have been born someone else!

I'm Not My Older Brother

I'm not my older brother
So please do not compare
To treat me as another
Would surely be unfair
He has ways of doing things
Ways that are his own
He's okay, but there's no way
That I'll become his clone
I'm not my older brother
And I do not wish to be
I'm happy to be who I am
And that is simply me.

Lesson 33

As people age, their bodies often become frail, but their wisdom strengthens. Discuss with students some typical physical characteristics of old people. Also discuss the fact that because elderly people tend to appear fragile, we often forget about or overlook their value. Older people have so many stories, so much wisdom, and so much knowledge to share. Have students share stories of their own grandparents or other elderly people they have known and loved and from whom they have learned. You may even choose to have students conduct an interview with an elderly person who lived through a certain historical time or event.

I Remember Grandpa

His bones were sort of creaky
His walk was really slow
His face was lined with wrinkles
His voice—a tremolo
Yet wiser than an owl
And stronger than an oak
I "heard" it when he smiled at me
I "felt" it when he spoke
And I think I know the reason now
That he appeared so old
His strength had left his body
And gone straight into his soul.

Lesson 34

The child in this poem is learning one of life's tough lessons. Lies tend to grow, and they always come back full circle to haunt us. Not only do they hurt us, but they also have the potential to hurt others. Have the students discuss lies—what they are, what might tempt people to tell them, what some of their possible consequences may be, etc. The issue of "trust" usually surfaces here. Regardless of what surfaces, however, this poem always makes for an interesting discussion with students!

I Told a Lie

I told a lie to you
You thought that it was true
You spread it around
It went all over town
And grew and grew and grew
Someone said it to someone else
Who said it to others, too
Then one of the others told my mother
So now what will I do?

Lesson 35

This poem is about second chances. Discuss with your students the fact that we all make mistakes and that mistakes can provide us with opportunities to learn and grow. We get many "second chances" in life. Allow students to share some of the mistakes they have made in life and the lessons they have learned from them.

You may also want to discuss the fact that second chances are not guaranteed in life. For instance, someone who drives recklessly and kills someone else does not get a second chance to make it up to that person. So the note of caution here is to think before you act because all of your actions have very definite consequences.

Young Again

There once was an old lady
Who was very, very mean
A more evil, wicked person
No one had ever seen
She walked outside one summer day
And a magic bee stung her
And then as she awoke each day
She started getting younger
At first she was eighty
And then seventy-nine
Seventy-eight, seventy-seven, seventy-six,
      seventy-five
Each day, a year behind
Soon she was a kid again
And once again in school
She sat beside her grandchildren
Who thought it pretty "cool"
Fourth grade, then third grade
Second grade, then first
Younger and younger she became
And began to fear the worst
So she found the magic bee again
And told it of her fear
If she got any younger
She would surely disappear
The bee agreed to sting her
Not once this time, but twice
She's getting very old again
But this time, she's nice.

About the Author

Annette Breaux is one of the most entertaining and informative authors and speakers in the field of education. She leaves her audiences with practical and doable techniques to implement in their classrooms immediately. Administrators agree that they see results from their teachers the next day.

Her message is one of practicality and personality in teaching, of feeling and healing in touching students' lives, and of common sense and creative teaching strategies. Her writings and presentations generate instant impact on the relationships between teachers and students.

A former classroom teacher and curriculum coordinator, she now serves as the Teacher Induction Coordinator for Nicholls State University in Thibodaux, Louisiana. She is the author of the FIRST Program, a new teacher induction program hailed as one of the best in the country.

Annette's expertise is in student achievement, classroom management, and new teacher induction. She is the author of *101 Answers for New Teachers and Their Mentors* and coauthor with her sister Elizabeth Breaux of *REAL Teachers, REAL Challenges, REAL Solutions*. She also coauthored a book with Dr. Harry Wong entitled *New Teacher Induction: How to Train, Support and Retain New Teachers*

Her down-south warmth, infectious humor, and ability to touch the hearts and souls of educators invariably bring audiences to their feet. Teachers who have read Annette's writings or heard Annette speak agree that they walk away with user-friendly information, heartfelt inspiration, and a much-needed reminder that they truly have chosen the most noble of all professions teaching.

You may contact Annette at abreaux@eyeoneducation.com